More Professional Tools

SEARCH & RESCUE
TOOLS

ANDERS HANSON

Consulting Editor, Diane Craig, M.A./Reading Specialist

A Division of ABDO

ABDO
Publishing Company

visit us at www.abdopublishing.com

Published by ABDO Publishing Company, a division of ABDO,
P.O. Box 398166, Minneapolis, Minnesota 55439. Copyright © 2014
by Abdo Consulting Group, Inc. International copyrights reserved in all
countries. No part of this book may be reproduced in any form without
written permission from the publisher. Super SandCastle™
is a trademark and logo of ABDO Publishing Company.

Printed in the United States of America,
North Mankato, Minnesota
102013
012014

 PRINTED ON RECYCLED PAPER

Editor: Liz Salzmann
Content Developer: Nancy Tuminelly
Photo Credits: Shutterstock

Library of Congress Cataloging-in-Publication Data

Hanson, Anders, 1980-
  Search & rescue tools / Anders Hanson.
    pages cm. -- (More professional tools)
  Audience: Ages 5-10.
  ISBN 978-1-62403-075-8
1. Rescues--Juvenile literature. 2. Assistance in emergencies--Juvenile
literature. I. Title.
  RA645.5.H363 2014
  362.18--dc23
                    2013022538

Super SandCastle™ books are created by a team of professional
educators, reading specialists, and content developers around five
essential components—phonemic awareness, phonics, vocabulary,
text comprehension, and fluency—to assist young readers as they
develop reading skills and strategies and increase their general
knowledge. All books are written, reviewed, and leveled for guided
reading, early reading intervention, and Accelerated Reader®
programs for use in shared, guided, and independent reading and
writing activities to support a balanced approach to literacy
instruction.

CONTENTS

MEET A RESCUER!

WHAT DOES A RESCUER DO?

A rescuer's job is to save people in danger. Sometimes people get lost, trapped, hurt, or **stranded.** It's a rescuer's job to find them and bring them to a hospital.

WHY DO RESCUERS NEED TOOLS?

Tools help rescuers find missing people and move them to safety.

3

Patrol Boat

Rescue Dog

Helicopter

Stretcher

HELICOPTER

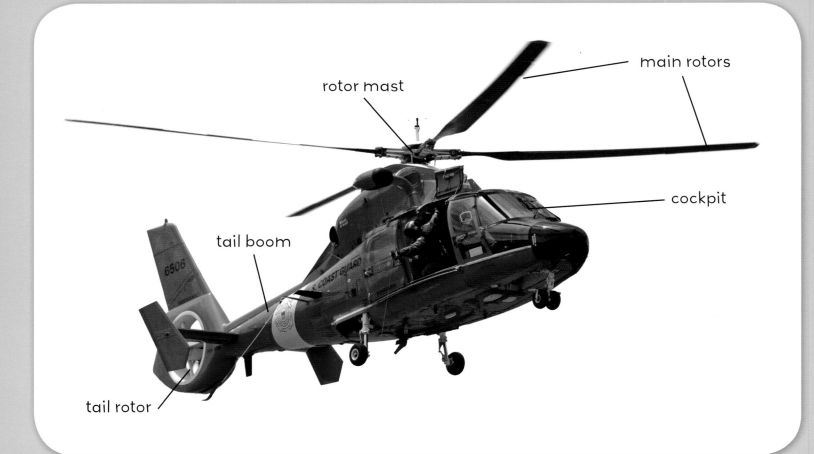

rotor mast

main rotors

cockpit

tail boom

6506

COAST GUARD

tail rotor

Helicopters can go places other vehicles can't.

Helicopters can fly low and slow. That helps rescuers find and rescue people more easily!

Helicopters are easier to control than airplanes. They can go places that don't have roads. They can also fly over water to search for people below.

Ted is a rescuer. He is being lowered from a hovering helicopter.

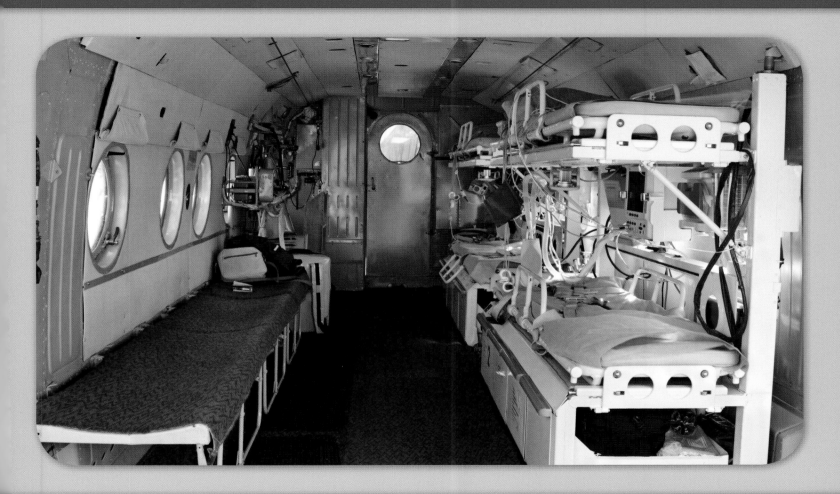

Some helicopters have **medical equipment** on board.
Doctors and nurses use it to treat people right away.

RESCUE DOG

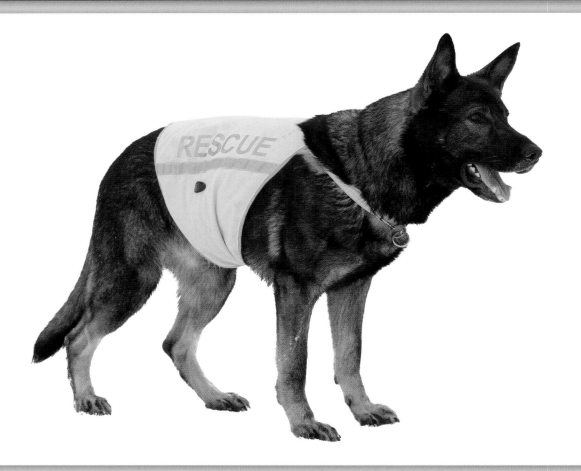

Rescue dogs use their keen senses to find missing people.

Dogs have a great sense of smell. Dogs can smell many things that people can't.

Rescue dogs use their noses to find people trapped beneath **rubble** or snow.

Tucker is training to become a rescue dog.
He will work with a search and rescue team.

Bella smells somebody trapped under the snow.
It's time to start digging!

STRETCHER

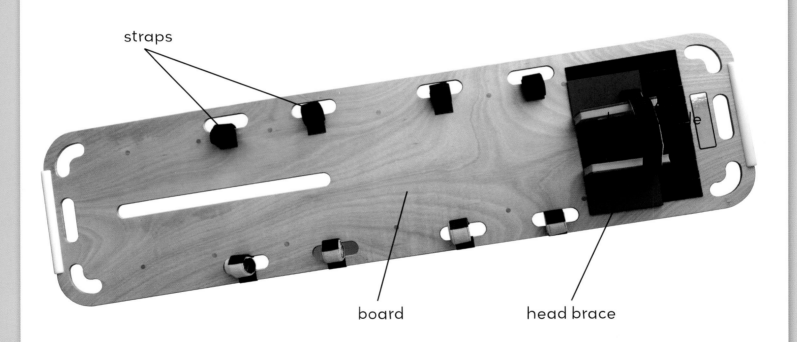

straps

board

head brace

Stretchers allow hurt people to be moved safely.

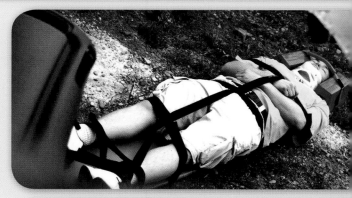

Injuries may become worse when the person is moved. To prevent this, hurt people are tied to a stretcher.

Stretchers keep the body and head still while the person is moved to a hospital.

Nate is rescuing a man who fell off a cliff. He tied the man to a stretcher. Then the man is lifted to safety.

Anna was trapped in an **avalanche**.
A rescue team carries her on a stretcher.

RESCUE BOAT

Rescue boats help people and ships stranded at sea.

Many different types of boats are used for search and rescue. Some are small **inflatable** boats. Others are huge ships.

The U.S. Coast Guard operates most of the rescue boats in the United States.

When a boat rescues someone who needs immediate medical attention, a helicopter is called in.

Some boats rescue large ships, not people.
They are called tugboats. They are small but powerful.

MATCH THE WORDS TO THE PICTURES!

The answers are on the bottom of the page.

MATCH GAME

1. rescue dog

a.

2. rescue boat

b.

3. helicopter

c.

4. stretcher

d.

TEST YOUR TOOL KNOWLEDGE!

The answers are on the bottom of the page.

1.
Helicopters can fly low and slow.

TRUE OR FALSE?

2.
Rescue dogs use their noses to find people trapped under snow.

TRUE OR FALSE?

3.
Stretchers stretch out a person's body.

TRUE OR FALSE?

4.
The U.S. Navy operates most of the rescue boats in the United States.

TRUE OR FALSE?

TOOL QUIZ

Answers: 1) true 2) true 3) false 4) false

23

GLOSSARY

avalanche – a large amount of snow, dirt, or rock sliding down a mountain.

equipment – a set of tools or items used for a special purpose or activity.

inflatable – able to be filled with air or another gas.

injury – a wound or other kind of harm or damage.

medical – having to do with doctors or health.

rubble – the rough, broken stones or bricks that are left after a building falls down.

ski – to glide on narrow strips of wood, metal, or plastic attached to one's feet.

strand – to force a boat onto the shore, or to leave someone somewhere without a way to leave.

strap – a narrow strip of leather or cloth used to tie things together.

vehicle – something used to carry people or large objects. Examples include cars, trucks, boats, and airplanes.